several years into writing
i decided against my work
and what i read i did not like
so i took all my papers
into our office at midnight
turning on the shredder
i shoved my work inside
the loss at the time didn't hurt
but now those pieces i can never recover
and down the drain went my effort
several weeks went by
then suddenly it occurred to me and i realized
i have some backed up on a flash drive
and that's why i have most of them remembered
i'm happy with the few i could find
and those i then transferred
but i wish i could go back in time
find me and try to stop her
from destroying those rhymes
because now i can no longer
be witness to my progress that i
am slowly but surely getting better

Dedicated to First,
Thank you for inspiring and cheering me on always,
I hope I can do the same for you,
Sincerely,
Second

CONTENTS

Dead Flowers Are Still Pretty   1

I Didn't Reciprocate   2

Trying   3

Not Just Another New Year's Resolution   4

Self-induced Insomnia   5

You'll Tell Your Mom A Different Story   6

I'd Never Be Content   7

Bleach   8

Saudade   9

Liar Liar   10

Some Things Are Just Meant To End   11

Writer's Block   12

"You'll Grow Out Of It"   14

Say Something. Please.   15

I Don't Like Texting   16

It Starts And Ends With You   17

From The Bottom Of My Heart, Screw You   18

The Human Chameleon   19

Contents

Pen And Paper ... 20

One Year ... 21

I Am Full Of Spiders ... 22

My Elastic Broke ... 24

Obligation Free ... 25

FOMO At Your Own Party ... 26

Let's Watch A Movie From Home Today ... 27

Falling From The Ground ... 28

Sinking From The Sky ... 30

Good Thing It Was Just A Star, Right? ... 32

Your Happiness Is Not Up To Me ... 33

Dollar Bills Dollar Signs ... 34

Old Habits Die Hard ... 35

Bad Haircut ... 36

Different Kind Of Different ... 37

Playing By Ear ... 38

Once A Theater Kid Always A Theater Kid ... 39

Bettering Yourself For Others ... 40

Banana Popsicles ... 41

Getting Over It ... 42

dead flowers are still pretty

i was at my cousin's house when i saw
in the kitchen, a vase full of wilted flowers.
"i like your irises," i say in an awe
"they're dead," she said, looking at the counter

"dead flowers are still pretty," i replied,
the brown leaves hadn't began to fall yet.
"that's oddly poetic," she smiled.
i grimly laugh and think, 'it is, isn't it?'

i didn't reciprocate

your head
in the clouds
filled with dread
don't look down
your imagination soars
but your dreams don't fly
we don't talk anymore

birds don't have feathers
fish don't swim
the sky rains, never
the light becomes dim
you wanted me at your door
but my feelings begged to differ
and now we don't talk anymore

trying

i am a sinner
my visions starting to falter
for this horror
Christ died on the alter

not just another New Year's resolution

will this year be different?
last year of waiting
last year of myself i'm hating?
can i stop worrying about the judgement?

will we grow further?
will my childhood issues shrink?
can i manage to rewire the way i think?
perhaps we will grow closer

or maybe things will get worse
and i will digress
or maybe i'll stay like this
and remain disfigured

i'm sick of feeling this way
so i'll try something new
for this next year to get through
tomorrow's a new day

only the future will tell
not going to lie
i'm really excited
to myself i say farewell

self-induced insomnia

four cups of coffee
each morning to get by
so drained each day
but peaking at midnight
i'm sipping more tea
because i'm sleep deprived
now i have to drug myself
to get any shut eye

i'm getting so angry
at this restless routine
but i understand
my lack of energy
falls upon the fact
i'm too caffeinated to sleep
the self-induced insomnia
falls upon nothing but me

you'll tell your mom a different story

my concern for you began to wilt
alongside my entire body
i was soon to leave for good
and i wanted to take you with me

using every ounce of strength
i wrapped your legs in my vines
you fell to the ground
and i wanted you to feel us die

you cried out begging
but my deaf ears wouldn't hear
i was pent up for so long
i didn't even shed a tear

i'd never be content

sometimes i want to crawl out of myself
judge me through not my own eyes
and see what they see
but i know deep down its just a waste
i know i'd never be satisfied
if i am what i wanted, i cannot believe

bleach

rag and brush in hand
i can tune out everything
scrubbing the corners of my mind
taking it out on the bathroom sink
while simultaneously not thinking at all
physically and mentally thoroughly cleaning
this is how i reset
removing every stain with bleach
the fog starts to fade
as i dust every nook and cranny
i feel so much better
with a clean home i can finally breathe

saudade

yes, i'll take what i can have
but coming to your place is still foreign
singing in your car is now bizarre
you started to sing a different chorus

i just wish i could stop comparing
what is in my head as "better times"
i see you struggling
and it's hard to watch from the sidelines

it's sad that it's not the same anymore
but i know should be happy, too
deep down i think i'm just sad
i'm not right there with you.

liar liar

liar liar
heart on fire
our fate
becoming dire
i can't see
choking on what we used to believe
"that person that nobody desires"
liar liar
heart on fire
it's far too late
now i'm wired
of this game
do you ever tire
liar liar
heart on fire
you i never wanted to hate
so it's a shame it turned out this way
i'd stay clear if i knew prior
that you were
a liar liar

some things are just meant
to end

the dried out rose
lying on my car's dash
was still there from graduation
falling apart, it had to go
so i tossed it into the trash
and had a revelation
this i already know
but not everything is meant to last
even if it's my rear view's reflection

writer's block

there is nothing i dislike more
than an unfinished poem
i talk so much about writing
but yet nothing to show them

"i'm still working on it,"
more like a bad case of writers' block
hunched at my desk trying to progress
the only thing moving is the clock
so i force it to completion
and now the rhyming's a bit odd

now i despise it
i hate using filler words
i want to do my best
so i don't cut corners

it was going so well
i hate to let down the buildup
i swear it true
it was on the tip of my tongue
that final last thought
i was so close to saying it was done

perhaps i'll try again tomorrow
cut myself some slack
i worked really hard
and maybe it will come back

so i close my notebook
and that moment is when
i close my eyes
and pull from within
when it seems to fit together
it all abruptly

"you'll grow out of it"

maybe if i take a hammer
to my dreams
they will shatter
and i will no longer
be cruelly deceived
by what i once believed

say something. please.

i've been left on read
my text messages are blue
i'm getting tired of this
i just wanted to talk to you

i don't like texting

why did you put a period after 'yes'?
are you mad, worried, or stressed?
i will pick apart what i have read
every word and comma i will dissect
but it's probably not what you meant
deep down i know you have good intent
and i know i'm overthinking this
so maybe i'll just try to go back to bed

it starts and ends with you

you'd beg me to see you
and because we were close, i went
you told me what you wanted HIM to do
then switch the roles of HIM to ME instead.
i guess you thought i wanted that, too
so that might explain why you did what you did
you got me alone in your room
we were just supposed to go to bed
that night, i barely slept through!
it was more than i could deal with
and that's really why i left you.

from the bottom of my heart, screw you

can't tell if you heard me or not
because you turned your read receipts off
perhaps i should be happy i'm not blocked
but your auto caps is now back on
and it hasn't even been that long
somehow you've already change a lot
i's are not dotted and t's aren't crossed
seemingly never gave a second thought
still, i reached out if you wanted to talk
yet you never checked on me at all
turns out, 'us' was something i'd never want
now my memories of you are filled with rot
when i realized the truth, i felt no loss
and whatever i saw in you is now gone

The Human Chameleon

i am the Human Chameleon
in a crowd, i twist and bend
my personality and then
i match them of their own skin
although, sometimes i can't help it
i'm too good at being a shapeshift
what if i don't want to blend?
what if it's a toxic place to be in?
i never had the time to comprehend
or else i would've never played pretend

pen and paper

i choose my implement
and let my pen flow onto my paper
until i drench my page with ink
and a drop rolls down my arm as i waver

it's not a plea
it's a form of expression
not at all one for others
they aren't to witness the affliction

i shelter others from my 'work'
i fear what they might believe
they'd be right, though
they wouldn't misconceive

my pen doesn't erase that well
my writing is persistent
it doesn't budge
it was a mistake i'll have to live with

it was stupid
but things are what they are
it was in the heat of the moment
and i shouldn't have pressed so hard.

one year

i feel it in my chest
a hollowed out feeling
that someone stole a lung
i try to take a breath
now i'm wincing
what have i become?

i am full of spiders

if you were to open me
i promise you wont find honeybees
no buttercups or flower seeds
but rather cobwebs and weeds
full of dead gnats and tiny beasts

if i passed here today
not much would actually change
my 'lifelessness' would be the same
all the time i feel this way
so why should i want to stay?

you say it's in my head
i say i'm already dead
why is this something you can't accept?
surprised to see a hollow wasp nest?
what else did you expect?
i told you i was full of insects!
even if i could feel again
there is no difference then
between being emotionally numb
and to now what i have become

even if what was inside came to life
i would still be full of termites
filled with live, giant horse flies
at this point and time
what once drew the line
has been completely divided
does it matter what's inside?
whether i'm full of dead versus alive?
you're sightless, being an outsider
you can't see, i'm still a host, full of spiders.

my elastic broke

my favorite bracelet
one of my own creation
had lettered beads
that read "filled with determination"

i was removing the band
when the elastic tore
and i watched my hope
scatter on the floor

my heart dropped to my stomach
my emotions had been building horribly
and my bracelet breaking
only rubbed in the irony

and just as my band had snapped
so did i lose my temper
with friends and those around me
i had been so filled with anger

obligation free

i fill my notes with words
rhyming, mismatched
but you don't want to feel my burn
to my stories you were never attached
please read them on your own terms
and not just because i ask

FOMO at your own party

why aren't i laughing?
this is supposed to be fun
why can't i feel much of anything?
why can't i be smiling
as much as everyone?
i catch all the jokes and puns
so why was it not as funny
as it was to everybody?
this is supposed to be
my own party
so why do i get a feeling
like i am watching a TV
a conversation play out in front of me
not completely
gone or dissociated,
still being involved
but not included
i always thought
i was an extravert
but now i want
nothing but
to take the closest exit

let's watch a movie from home today

i have a hard time relaxing
staring at the bright, large screen
so i clutch the arm on the theater's seat
as my mind conjures a tragedy
one of a mass shooting
killing my loved ones and family
looking around, all i see
blood the color of cherry candies
gunshots like kernels bursting
then suddenly i'm launched back into reality
and i've managed to miss twenty minutes of the movie

falling from the ground

everyday is the same
body on autopilot
brain on a different wave
detached from the physical
yet everyone else feels the change

i'm sinking up to the sky
my grips so gone
weeks and months pass by
but my routine remains
and in the clouds i collide

on the earth once again and
i decide a different path
i'm trying, i really am
but it's difficult to avoid
the traps of sinking sand

can't grip onto gravity
so i stumble again
forget about reality
i'm disappearing
and a lost personality

i think i'm upside down
am i doing what's right?
doesn't matter, i'm sky bound
i look up to see that i
am falling from the ground

sinking from the sky

this is a pretty bizarre in-between
i am stuck in the blue
at least that's what it seems
i pass the exosphere
and i now cannot breathe

now down in space
i frantically glance around
searching for a familiar face
but there is nothing but stars
of humanity there is no trace

now i pass by Saturn
here completely alone
and i feel it getting worse
i wave to Pluto
as everything gets colder

just as i think i'll be here for eternity
i twice see the little dipper
am i reentering the galaxy?
i'm now in the opposite direction
though i never did a one-eighty

i'm flying back to the surface
can i manage to change this time?
another chance to adjust?
i just want to feel again
will i be able to beat this?

and shooting all the way up
back to the dirt
here i come
feet exactly where
i first fell from.

good thing it was just a star, right?

tonight when i got out of my car
up in the sky, i saw a shooting star
almost as if waiting for this very moment
i shot up my wish in the sky in an instant
looking closer into the night
i saw that my "star" was just a satellite
at my mistakes i couldn't help but laugh
is what i wished for something i really want back?

your happiness is not
up to me

i understand it's useless now
looking for an answer
that does not exist
i no longer need
to rip up my innards
i'm allowed to resist
it's not my issue to resolve
you're not mine to be "fixing"
so i can now leave this

dollar bills dollar signs

dollar bills dollar signs
is that all what matters?
what i can make before i die?
forget about a heartfelt legacy
it's the money i leave behind
simply existing to pay rent
is not truly living a life
can one even make a living
solely off of rhymes?
surely not these days
it's silly to say i want to write
but i refuse to disregard the draw
i will not be confined

old habits die hard

to lose our friendship, i feared nothing greater
and honestly, if you weren't so perverse
i daydream that we could have recovered
but you chose to stay immature
how things happened was nothing i preferred
and i tell everyone you were someone i got over
clearly, it's not something i can ensure
because, despite how much you made me hurt
i still end up putting your birthday on my calendar

bad haircut

a week ago, i got a haircut
but i didn't like how it looked
i didn't feel pretty
it didn't feel me
and it made me worry
worry that others opinions
of previous ones given
would change and go back
because of now of what i lacked
but not only that
the most important judgement
the very cause of this lament
was of my very own belief
and it was my reality
it was hard to like me
but now in hindsight
i see my thinking wasn't right
others have it much worse
and i know i will recover
and myself i got over
swallowing my ignorant fears
i knew it would grow out in half a year

different kind of different

a hole from your heart to your head
are you braindead?
what i would do to walk around your mind
any place, any time

as i take my step
i prepare for land
not the lack of depth

confusion is what i expected
but to my surprise
in your emptiness
i nearly suffocated
your light is real but brief
a thought process
vast beyond belief

how in this condition do you stay?
as i leap i will ask to take your hand
so we both can find a new way

playing by ear

one early morning
when i was home alone
i crept into my parents room
and sat at the piano
i opened the bench
finding the books i used to know
i cracked my knuckled and tried to play
but i failed to read any notes
i tried to recall
but the keys let out a nasty sound
like nails on a chalkboard
in the noisy mess i nearly drowned
taking off my hands
i folded my arms and frowned
then i put my old books away
and tried something so profound
a catchy melody
one in my head for so long
the tune was stuck inside
so by ear i played the song
the keys flowed smoothly
so i began to sing along
with no book guiding me
how could i possibly play wrong?

once a theater kid always a theater kid

it was a few hours before our wedding
going through one last practice for our day
and we were about to exchange rings
so i had to pass on my bouquet
good thing we were just practicing
because i contorted myself in an odd way
to give my flowers to my bridal party
"that looked a bit strange"
commented my family
"i was just trying not to turn away
and keep my body open facing"
a groomsmen, familiar with the stage
replied, "i knew exactly what you were doing"

bettering yourself
for others

me and a couple friends started daily
exercise, a way to better our beings
eating more regularly
moving ourselves, but not excessively
improving our minds' relationship with our bodies
and one day, while we were stretching
i poised an interesting question
"did you make any New Year's resolutions?
if so, how are you doing on them?"
my question seemed relevant
after all, we were working on self-improvement
and after a few minutes
she replied with
"gesturing with my palm in conversation
rather than pointing since it's subtly passive aggressive"
and i thought to myself
'i wish i could have that kind of self-awareness'
and i believe that her resolution is the true definition
of what it really means to be selfless
such a small gesture, yes
but it's the thought process
that makes the effort so important
so now i gesture, with not a finger pointed
but rather with an open palm, lifted

banana popsicles

we went to the store and i let you choose
a frozen treat of banana popsicles
to the house we brought them to
eating them to cool ourselves while
both of us sorted through
boxes and moved the furniture
at my residence, some place new
and you kept reassuring me
that this was something i could do
that was last summer
i bought them again this afternoon
i can't really taste much besides sugar
but i am reminded of sweet memories of you

getting over it

i used to bite my fingernails
pinch and pull skin tags
bite the skin off my lip
and pick at my eyelashes
these things were built into me
all terrible, nervous habits

i finally managed to free myself
it was a difficult task
and it took several years
but finally, at last
my success was signified
by my nails growing back

FALLING FROM THE GROUND